Neat Cursive Writing

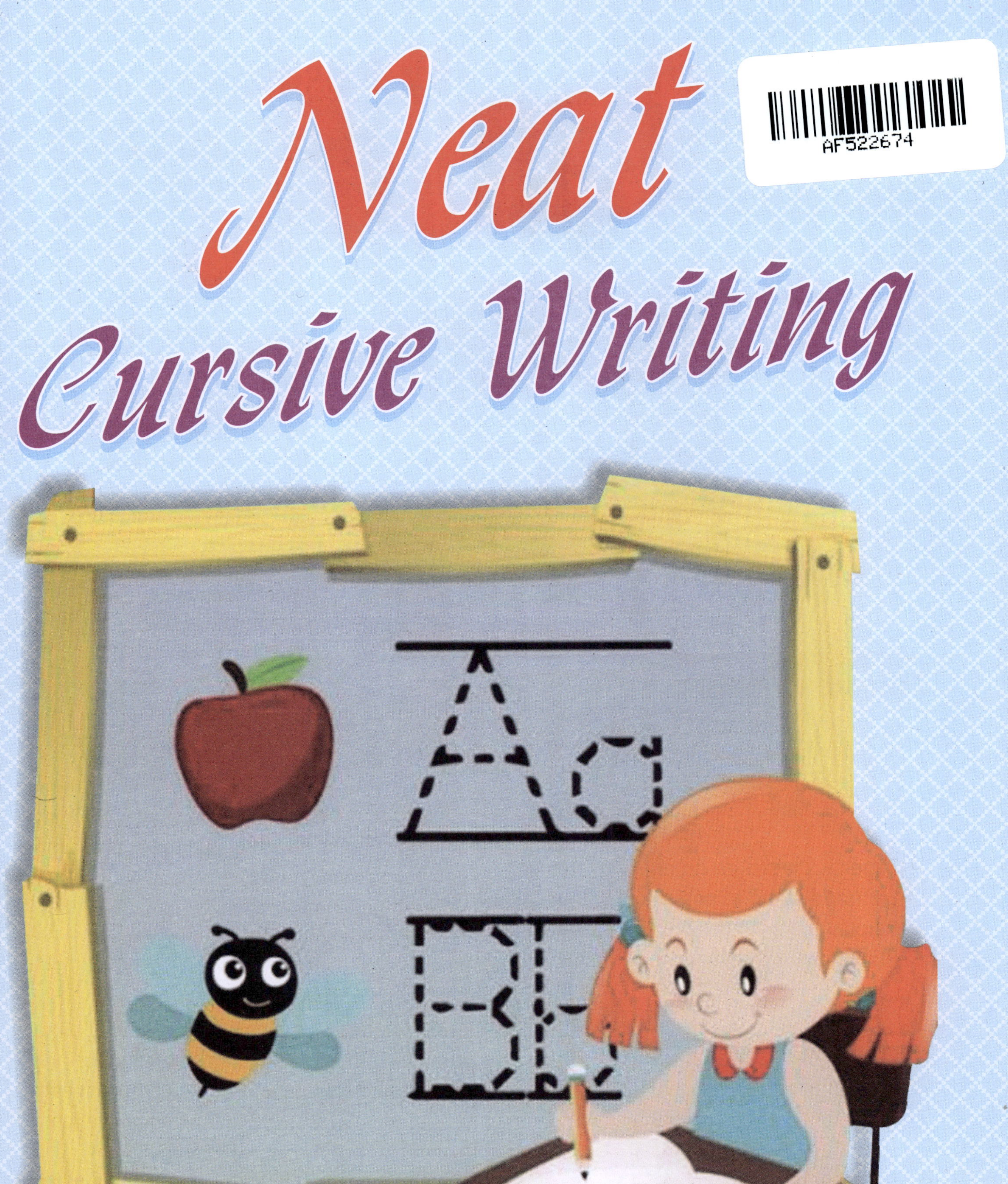

Hand and Body Position

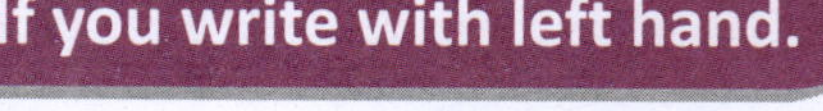

Paper is placed on an angle to the right . Right hand steadies the paper and moves it up as you near the bottom of the page. Left hand is free to write.

If you write with right hand.

Paper is placed on an angle to the left . Lefthand steadies the paper and moves it up as you near the bottom of the page. Right hand is free to write.

Hold the pencil loosely about 1/2 to 1" above the sharpened point. Hold it between your thumb and index (pointer) finger. Let it rest on your middle finger. Do not grip the pencil tightly or your hand will become very tired. Do not let your hand slip down to the sharp point or you will have difficulty in writing properly.

We see birds on the tree.

We see birds on the tree.

Cricket is my favourite game.

Cricket is my favourite game.

India is a democratic country.

India is a democratic country.

Practice makes the man perfect.

Practice makes the man perfect.

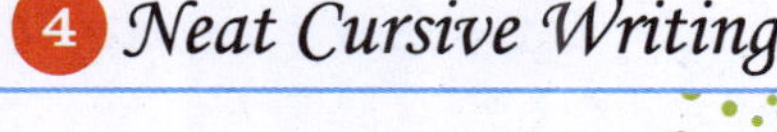

God is kind to all.

God is kind to all.

Variety is the spice of life.

Variety is the spice of life.

A proper study of mankind.

A proper study of mankind.

Gentleness is better than force.

Gentleness is better than force.

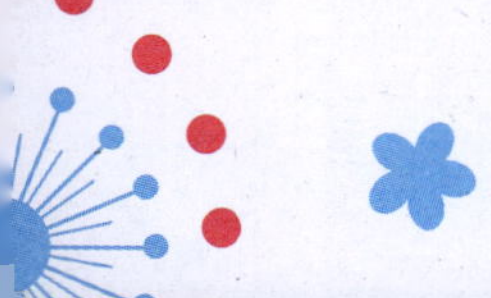

Never take your pride in your riches.

Never take your pride in your riches.

Every cloud has a silver lining.

Every cloud has a silver lining.

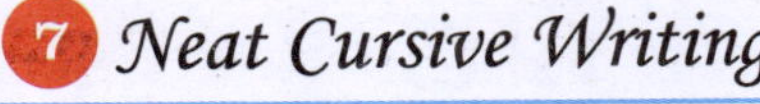

Better alone than in a bad company.

Better alone than in a bad company.

Moderation gives charm to life.

Moderation gives charm to life.

Trees give us oxygen and timber.

Trees give us oxygen and timber.

Stone walls do not make a prison.

Stone walls do not make a prison.

Morning walk is a good exercise.

Morning walk is a good exercise.

An honest man is always fearless.

An honest man is always fearless.

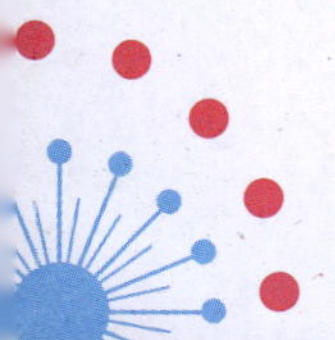

Time is the greatest innovator.

Time is the greatest innovator.

We must learn to hear the truth.

We must learn to hear the truth.

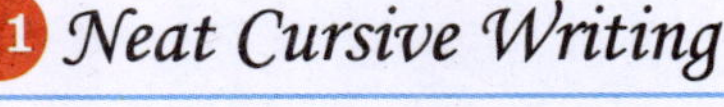

Ashoka was a great king.

Ashoka was a great king.

Truth shines as a star.

Truth shines as a star.

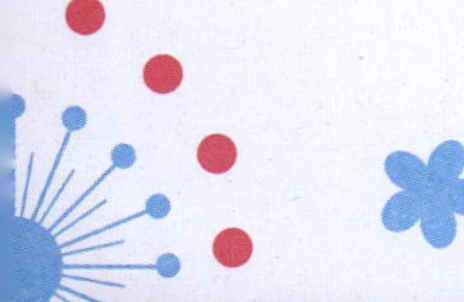

Tulsidas wrote the Ramayana.

Tulsidas wrote the Ramayana.

Realist believes in the realism.

Realist believes in the realism.

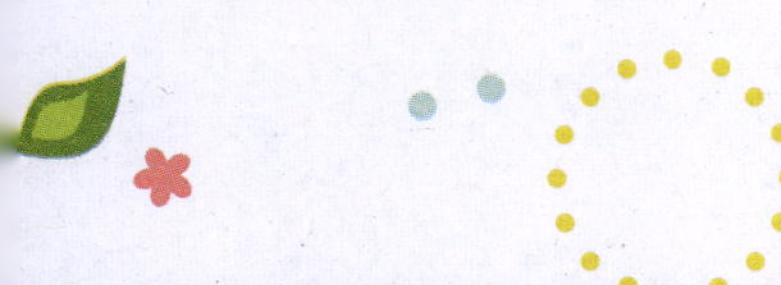

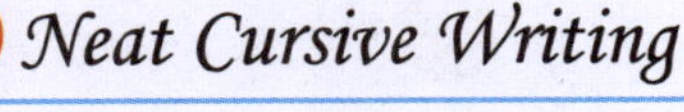

A mother's love is selfless.

A mother's love is selfless.

Freedom is our birth right.

Freedom is our birth right.

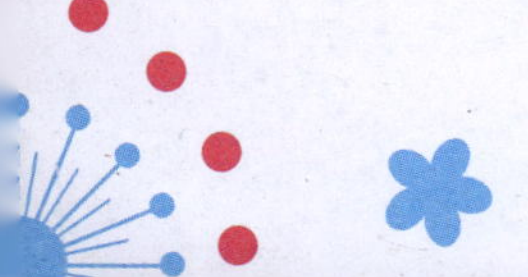

As you sow, so shall you reap.

As you sow, so shall you reap.

Long absent, soon forgotten.

Long absent, soon forgotten.

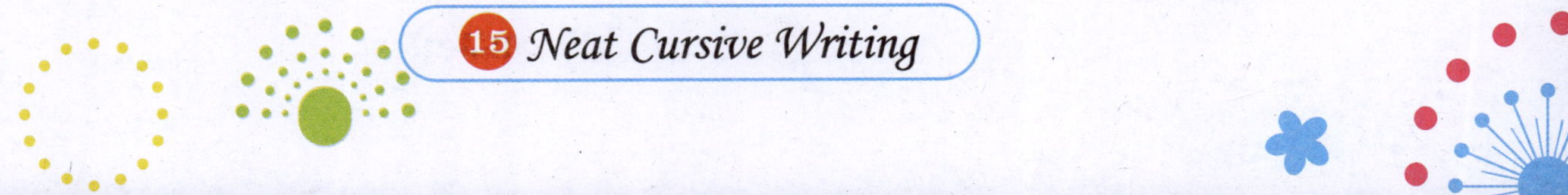

Give and take is a fair play.

Give and take is a fair play.

The earth moves round the sun.

The earth moves round the sun.

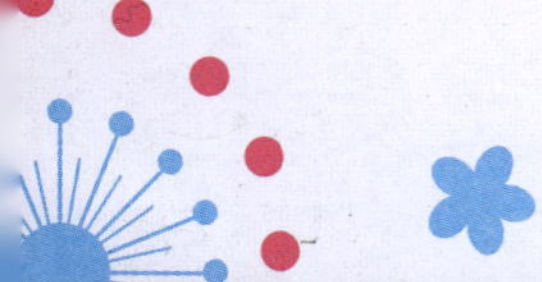

Ostrich is the bird that cannot fly.

Ostrich is the bird that cannot fly.

Where there is a will, there is a way.

Where there is a will, there is a way.

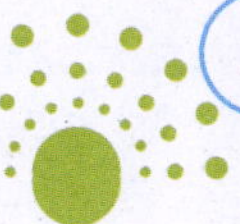

Kindness is never goes unrewarded.

Kindness is never goes unrewarded.

Never give up hope in despair.

Never give up hope in despair.

Boat sails in the river.

Boat sails in the river.

The army defends our country.

The army defends our country.

Postman delivers the letters.

Postman delivers the letters.

An artist paints the picture.

An artist paints the picture.

Gardner waters the plants.

Gardner waters the plants.

Watch tells us the time.

Watch tells us the time.

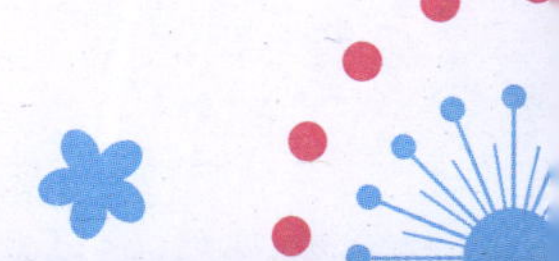

The sun gives us sunlight.

The sun gives us sunlight.

Trees help to bring rain.

Trees help to bring rain.

A week has seven days.

A week has seven days.

Morning is the time of rising sun.

Morning is the time of rising sun.

Noon is the time of burning sun.

Noon is the time of burning sun.

Evening is the time of setting sun.

Evening is the time of setting sun.

Night is the time of hiding sun.

Night is the time of hiding sun.

Books are our true friends.

Books are our true friends.

Good children obey their parents.

Good children obey their parents.

Hockey is our national game.

Hockey is our national game.

Cricket is a popular game.

Cricket is a popular game.

Hindi is our national language.

Hindi is our national language.

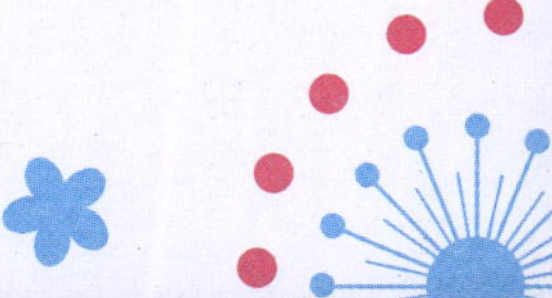

India has cycle of seasons.

India has cycle of seasons.

Its climate is very charming.

Its climate is very charming.

Spring is the king of seasons.

Spring is the king of seasons.

I like the spring season the most.

I like the spring season the most.

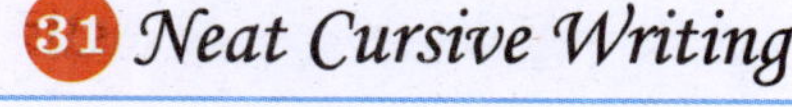

We enjoy this colourful earth with

our eyes. Eyes are the most

valuable organ in our body.

But how do we see? The

function of our eyes is very

complex. Our eyes have two

convex lenses. They produce reflection

on retinas. The retinas are positioned

just behind the lenses. The

black parts in the eyes are

the lenses. The reflection of a

a thing are always upside down.

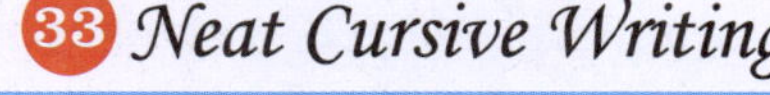

Once, a vast land of Russia was

ruled by a king. The king was

a great warrior. Moreover,

was a good king because he

loved his subjects. He was

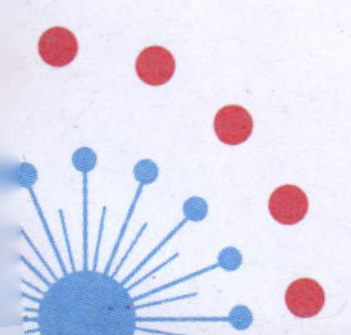

very kind and charitable. But the

king had one cruelty. The king used

to kill the barbers who came

to cut his hair. After cutting

the hair of the king, the

barber was killed instantly.

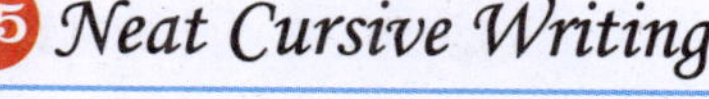

In the course of time. all the

barbers except a very old one were

killed. The king asked his men

to bring the old barber to cut

his hair. The barber came

and did his duty. After this,

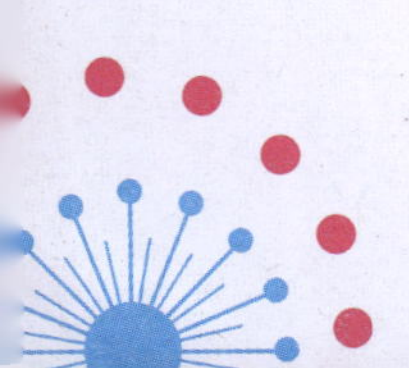

the king ordered to kill the barber.

But he prayed to spare his life. He

said, "Your Honour, if you

kill me then there will be

none to cut your hair." The

king became thoughtful. At last,

the king agreed on condition. The

king said, "Don't tell the secret

that you have learnt today

to anyone. If you reveal it,

you will beheaded immediately."

But the barber revealed the

secret. In sometime, the whole

kingdom learnt the secret. The news

came to the king and he

heard the same thing. He

ordered to kill that barber.

Now write a few lines about your aim in life.

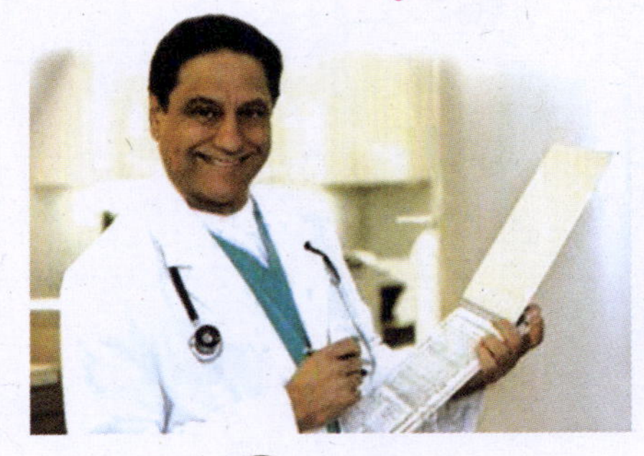

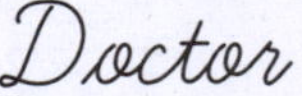

Doctor

Soldier

Photographer